Poetry

Emotions Released

Travis

ISBN: 978-1-4669-8031-0 (sc)
ISBN: 978-1-4669-8030-3 (e)

Trafford rev. 03/12/2013

 www.trafford.com

North America & international
toll-free: 1 888 232 4444 (USA & Canada)
phone: 250 383 6864 ♦ fax: 812 355 4082

Contents

Unknown feelings

I want to look in her eyes and lose myself to her
soul
I want to hold her in my arms to stay warm from
this cold
No feelings match what it is when I'm beside her
No wonder in the world can be more beautiful
than her
I have restless nights when she's not at my side
And each mornings wake has an empty feeling go
by
But then I see her in my hours of late
And I can kiss her with the passion we create
I don't know what to call this maybe it's love
But until I'm sure I will just sit beside her on this
cloud we float on above

Unrated Soldier

I'm an unrated soldier defective to the cause
I won't fight for this country because of all of it's
    wrongs
I refuse to lift a gun for the government no
    matter how much it needs me
Because every shot fired is more money to fuel
    their greed
But I'll die for my family and the people that I
    love
And I will keep climbing higher and dive down
    from above
That's what's worth dying for the people at home
But why leave the states unprotected and alone
That's why I silently fight here the unwanted
    fighter
Because on this soil they're starting a brand new
    fire

Soul of a Demon, Heart of a Man

Which am I really a demon or a man
I hate the pain of others but I can't ever make a
    stand
I get beaten and bruised but get back up for more
And the thought of useless killing makes me sick
    of this war
My anger grows strong but my compassion is
    stronger
And at the end of each day my world just gets
    darker
I have the soul of a demon but the heart of a
    good man
But no matter what I am I'm still not accepted in
    this land

No Time for Love

I want to love her but she says we don't have time
I want to see her but to do so just isn't right
Too much is stacked against us in this crazy
     world
Our paths never meet instead they curl
Right where I want to hold her and make her
     whole day bright
I would stay up and talk to her if it meant no
     sleep at night
But in the end there just isn't room her and me
And our lives grow apart farther than the greatest
     sea

Honesty

All I asked for was honesty
But instead I got lies
I work hard to live right
And try to get by
But I don't get a break
Even when I'm beaten down
I just stand up and take the punch
While everyone else stands around
People watch my pain and walk on
As if I were just a piece of trash
So now broken down and heartless
We will see how long I will last

Slipping Away

I would wait for you 'til the end if time
I would dream of you every night
I would wish for your smile on every star
I would wait to give you my own heart
But the times are cruel and our paths don't cross
Our bright sunny days in this world have been lost
I would bring them back if I could today
But I can't wait anymore since you let me slip away.

An Angel's Tears

Her beauty can only be matched by few
Her grace has her dancing on air
With every turn she sends the world in a trance
With every smile you'll melt at her feet
With eyes that hypnotize you to her will
And soul so kind you'll think she's an angel
This girl should find love with one devoted to
     her
So her tears can be chased far from her sight

Night's Alone

The nights alone take their toll
The cold wind blows across my hands
The sound of silence breaks my soul
The feeling of emptiness destroys my heart
Nothing breaks this curse of solitude
The nightmares of my mind take over reality
When alone I'm weak as a new born child
And the shadow takes over my will
But to others outside I try to look strong
I try to show no signs of pain
But at times I want to break down and shout
That this fate has taken all the light from me

Rage's Strike

The color red fills up my eyes
Raw emotion so strong I can't rest
The power in it is uncontrollable
There's no force in the world that can stop it
Rage so pure there is no thought
Twenty years of pain brought forth
No one can quell this beast
That has slowly taken over my heart
Now I feel the full pain set in
I hoped this day would never come
Broken heart and soul destroyed
I leave without a farewell to her

There's no apologies left to say
Just tears that drop like driving rain
On to the cheeks of a face that once was pure
And all the pain that she had to endure
Lie before her like a waiting predator
The fear of loss has fully taken her
She has nothing left and wants it to end
The person who did this left nothing to mend
Her broken heart the world now sees
And a soul so weak it's gone in the breeze
I want to lift her from this pain and make her
    better
I'd run to her to help her no matter the weather
No tornado or hurricane would stop me from
    getting to this dove
Because I will stop at nothing to show her true
    love

I've hidden you from the world
No eyes will find you in this place
I wish you to never rise
I wish for your power to stay encased
You're to dangerous to have around
Earthquakes seem like subtle shakes
The tears you'll bring to people
And all the hearts you'll break
But one day I will need you
It's getting closer I can feel it
So you'll be free once again
My warrior's spirit

I've lived in the shadows of everyone's lies
They fear to tell me the truth like they have
    everything to hide
I want the truth no matter how much it hurts
I can take the pain because lying hurts worse
If you think I'm angry you're sadly mistake
These lies pushed me off the edge because you
    have forsaken
My trust in you when I gave you it all
And now I see it wasted as I constantly fall
I write with my hear in all that I wrote
And just like the beginning my heart is now
    broke
That I can't trust you all go tell me the truth
And now my rage has finally take root
I say goodbye to you but it's not my end
This is where I leave your lies as I wished we
    were friends

She asked me one day for a decent man
That's when I got the courage to offer her my
    hand
I took a leap of faith to find some one to hold
Some one to trust someone to warm the cold
But I got a speech from her not even the truth
And it hurt so much down to my hearts root
A lie that she won't give me a chance because
    we're good friends
And she's afraid if we break up that friendship
    will end
But that turn from the truth broke the last part of
    me
And as the gates in me open all my emotions for
    her to see
Now she will see I don't hold hatred or anger
Only kindness and compassion, and also the
    potential to love her.

What does the dove say when you ask her to fly
She is stuck in her nest afraid to take to the sky
She wants to stay in safety resting in her bubble
She isn't interested in adventure when she'll
     get into trouble
The robin flies around diving and twisting
Trying his best to show her the life she's missing
He tries to ask her to take just one chance
A chance at a life that should be a never
     ending dance
But she is still afraid to leave her safe haven
And he understands for he's as wise as a raven
He'll wait patiently until she's ready to fly
That's when he'll ask her to join him in the sky.

The nights continue to grow darker every day
The pains grow stronger as I sleep
Nightmares rule my mind as the hours tic by
Nightmares so horrible that no mere
    words can describe
I beg and plead to all the gods for help
But my prayers go unheard
Now I just beg for the mornings to come
Or for an anchor to pull me back from the dark

How would your life be if you never met me?

I bet it would be grand spending every day at the
beach in the sand,

Looking at the people as they walk by and you'd
always have blue never grey skies.

Life with me around is nothing but pain and
confusion and all day I just stare at this
created delusion.

I want to just leave and have my memory
forgotten by you but how could I mean that
when I really do love you.

I feel this darkness looming over my heart

I fear I have no where else to run

I see the memories of you that I hold dear

That shine in my life like the golden sun

But as the darkness approaches your memories fade

I know I lost you this time for good

The light just leaves me as my heart cries out

The apology that was left misunderstood

Why has this happened when I asked for so little

Just one more season cycle to hold you in my arms

But even with divine power and will stronger
        than a human

It seems that as myself I lost all my charms

I don't feel like I'll make it so I'll just give up

There's nothing to a life in the darkness

I just want you to know that my heart is still
        yours

May it grant you a life with light and happiness

I wonder if people can really see
The demon stirring inside of me
Born from the hate and fear I give
Because that's the only way I live
I am subject to all their lies
And now they keep my hands in ties
But I always wonder if the really knew me
Would they truly fear that demon they see.

I lived my life day to day
Fighting with all my strength and words that I
    say
I run to my goals and dreams at the top
Only to be shot down no sound but the pop
I keep trying to make it beaten and bruised
Yet everyone still sees me as used
For the things that I do for everyone's doubts
But I keep on fighting the most impossible bouts
They all look and laugh as I lose my fights
Yet I keep going like a hawk in flight.
They finally ask why I continue though I fall
And I say "I never truly fail if I give it my all"

I've got the weight of the world upon my
    shoulders
Everyone expecting me to be their holder
Of the knowledge and answers to all of life
When I'm struggling my self just to make it by
I'm not strong enough for them to look up to
I'm not the savior they want just out of the blue
I've tried so hard to help them all
But in the end I just get thrown to the wall
Into a battle I've already fought
All the way back to apathetic thought
My anger tries to push them back
And the rage builds up ready to attack
This is the sign of me turning away
From a world so sad and full of dismay

Skies of grey loom over me
Sadness flows through me in waves
No body even cares for me
At the end of the day
All I am is a charity case
I'm someone they feel sorry for
Just a laugh for them all
At the end of the day
So now I disappear
Never to be seen again
They won't even miss me
At the end of the day

Tonight's the night I lose my bet,
Tonight's the night I drink to forget,
Tonight's the night I start my regret,
'Cause last night's the night I seemed to forget,
That I have feelings for you,
Those feelings came out of the blue,
Threatening to tear me from you,
So this is the path I choose,
So don't' be angry that I'm gone,
This realization hit me like a bomb,
And my will is drained away by this song.
Now this is the part where you tell me to stay
That through everything there is a better way,
But no matter what I still make this the day,
That I drain and wash your memory away

These feelings welled up so high,
Threatening to send these words to the sky,
The problem is within this heart of mine,
Now I'm hoping I can slip on by.
I don't want to make you thinks this is undying
     love,
No this is just the thought flown by the dove,
Maybe in time we can take these feelings above,
But until then I won't say it's love.
Yet I can't stand this feeling of just wanting
     to be around you,
Just seeing your brown eyes make my skies blue,
All I'll tell you is these feelings are true,
But for some reason I won't give you the clue.

I just want to give up I want to leave this place
But no matter what I do God throws me back to
    the base
Of this mountain of release from feelings and
    pain
Caused by this stress and un-relieving strain
Of heart ache and sorrow covering me like a
    dome
And my only relief is writing these poems
Yet I know I can't write and my rhymes are bad
It's just that sometimes it really makes me sad
To know that I'll end up alone
Friends aren't enough sometimes to guide me
    home
So I take my heart and toss it to the sky above
Cause right now I'm certain there's no such thing
    as love.

I have this gnawing feeling in my soul of being
    alone
I don't know why its there or even if its shown
All I know is my heart is filled with cracks
from all the lies spread around behind my back
I've tried to pick up the pieces and move on fast
Yet its impossible with the haunting memories of
    the past
I'm too broken to ever be whole
So I shun my feelings to darkness living like a
    mole
Will I ever see the light again I don't even know
All I'm certain of is this life can end with a simple
    blow
So weak and fragile makes me feel pathetic
and with me as the protector people just don't'
    get it
That I'm the one guy trying to right all the
    wrongs
But with a world filled with evil its an attack two
    pronged
So I just give up and let this world fall alone
For now I'm just content to live enough to make
    it home.

Sometimes I don't know what to do
I know I can talk the talk but don't have the
	moves
Every time I step closer my fear pushes me away
The fear I won't be good enough keeps these
	feelings at bay
When I'm around you words don't' come out
	right
Like there's a rope around my brain keeping my
	thoughts tied
So my jumbled words make me out to be a fool
Now with no chance of even a thought from you
I'm so weak and pathetic I should just live under
	the rocks
Just throw my life away and start living in a box
Or maybe just drink away this pain flowing in
	my chest
Knowing that you reject me before I take a breath
Now I just see darkness and no aim in my future
The blackness never stopping this void getting
	deeper
One day I'll be lost into it unable to return
That day is the day my memories will burn
And as you start to wish you took a chance with
	me
I will be lost in the dark abysmal sea.

And as I drift off to sleep waiting for the next day
Every word in my head preparing what to say
Now that I know these feelings are true
I so badly want to say how much I love you
So I'll give it time for you to decided
On if I'm worth giving a try
And even if I have to wait for the moon to turn
    blue
The wait will be worth it since this love is only
    for you

You asked me what I want from you, you asked
    me to be true
I answered I want your body and your lips with
    your mind too
I want your body to hold when you feel alone
I want your lips to meet mine in a kiss when I
    bring you home
I want your mind to fly with mine in our world
    no one can see
But in truth I couldn't be more happy to have just
    all of you with me

I have been used for my emotions to be a ladder
like I'm nothing but steps my thoughts and true
    feelings don't even matter
People want to test me on how angry I can get
or if I feel sorrow my tears come to bets
I don't know what people get out of it maybe a
    laugh
they probably think that all this anger will pass
but the more they press the higher it builds up
the pressure behind it threatens to blow up
the explosive nature enough to break me
the feelings all let out in a never ending sea
Of malice that will set in never backing down
The red anger in my eyes seems to make me
    drown
In the dark sea of no return
the insanity taking over starting to burn
a permanent place in my mine
while reason is left in a dark corner blind
this is what will happen if it continues
but you don't care cause I mean nothing to you

As blue sky's fade to black I stand at the at the
    edge of ruin and redemption,
I look back and wonder why I sacrifice all I am
    for such barbarians of the human race,
then I remind myself all I had to live for and all
    I was happy for was a smile and a laugh to
    grow in some hearts,
and that's when I jump into the black abyss not
    letting this world end with horror.

In every life there is a verse unsung
Mostly because of the battles not won
All because of the fatal flaw
And the death brought about in the carnivorous
    maw
Of the beasts in hell hungry for life
and those who fight will always lose their life
because if what they are protecting means more
    than the world
the life they have will be forfeit after the twirl
of clashing blades and fists alike
after the battle its a bloody midnight
but in the end you see its true
that the death of the hero brought skies of blue
Now its my turn to sacrifice it all
In this war on terror there will only be a fall
No way to back out or accept defeat
Too much is at stake if I let myself be beat
So in the end my sacrifice will save
and in history books it will speak about how
    brave
I was to stand alone against a world so evil and
    dark
and my heroic act was the beginning spark
But the fear I have of never seeing you again
is the unsung verse of my final end.

What am I supposed to do when my luck runs
    out
When I lose everything and everyone one I have?
Do I just sit there and cry about all the pain
Do I try to tell myself things aren't that bad?
It's my own damn fault for being to stubborn
It's all because I kept myself under the covers
I never moved out never tried to be on my own
And that's why I deserve to spend the rest of my
    life alone
I'm nothing but a failure at every single thing I
    try
And now I understand how everything happened
    and why
It's too late for me now to make all the right
    moves
But now that I know, I now have a path for me to
    choose.

Broken bloody and bruised
I can't stop all that I do
Because I fear of letting you down
I fear to see you turn around
I'm supposed to be strong and keep up this fight
But in the end I lose the true sight
What will happen when I turn black and blue
I know that it will be caused by what I do for you
And in the end I know you will demand more
Like I'm a broken soldier marching to the shore
So I stand here now broken bloody and bruised
All because I care too much to ever lose you

I can't sleep tonight because I can still see her
    face
I see her tears roll off her cheeks as age sets in
    this dark place
I try to consul her to take this pain away
But I'm to afraid to say a word in fear of being
    pushed away
What do you do for someone you could feel like
    this on sight
When their world turns dark what can I do to
    bring it to light

Would you think I'm weird if I said you're all
    that's on my mind
Would it be wrong if I said you're the only star
    that I see shine
Is it bad that I dream of your lips that I can kiss
Or the smell of the air as you walk in that I just
    can't miss
The sweet scent and bright smile are all I can
    think about
And a dream of you and me in a loving brace
Makes the world seem to stop and stay frozen for
    a minute
But every thought about you makes my heart
    race.

The first drink fills me but the thoughts of pain
    are still there
I buy a second to remember why I'm standing
    here
At the third my memories fill my mind like
    nightmares
And the fourth burns down my throat with less
    pain than what's in my heart
I try to drink a fifth but there's no way to forget
But I down it anyway just so it's something else
    I'll try to regret
Finally after seven or eight drinks I pay my tab
    and disappear from the bar
No trace of me being there except the tip left on
    the marble
And I drive away still filled with anger and regret
The memories still haunting my mind with past
    events
Before I know it I feel like all gravity is gone
The world seems to spin upside down
Then I find myself just lying off the side of the
    road
I just close my eyes full of tears not even trying
    to cry for help.

As the winter brings darkness and set in the cold
That's when you see the light of love fill the
    chilled air
The warmth of connected hearts heats up each
    home
The feeling of being held chases away any fears
But I stay alone through the frigid winds and
    dark night
But as I lie on my back in the open fields I see the
    beauty of the first snow's falling

I'm sorry to say that this is goodbye
I wished for one more dawn with you
But I'm afraid if I stay when the sun does rise
I'll be forever kept with you
In our heart we wish for nothing but happiness
In our dreams we wish for the world
But when that sun rises I'll wish for nothing more
Than for you to live life without a turn
Don't look back on what we used to be
Or look back on what we could have been
Just look forward into a bright new future
A new future where I don't exist

Come lie with me and help me chase away these
thoughts
Hold me close and chase away these dreams
Rest your head on my chest and chase away my
pain
Hold my hand in yours and chase away these
tears
Let your feet play with mine and chase away my
fears
Let your breath wash over me and chase away my
doubts
Let your lips touch mine and chase away all my
sorrow
Until I open my eyes and realize you were never
here

I wish to bid you a good morning on this
 beautiful day of grey
I wish to welcome you to this land of endless rain
A wasteland of broken dreams and wishes that
 haven't come true
Now that you're hear tell me a little more about
 you
Tell me which heart aches and pains you suffer to
 end up here
Which part of life you wish to give up that was
 so dear
And as you speak with me the clouds above you
 will have light shine through
A bright blue sky will break out making all of life
 seem brand new
And while I take away your pain my rain will
 beat down harder for a while
But I'm happy with that if in the end I was able to
 help you leave with that beautiful smile.

I guess this is the part where I put everything on
    the table
All my hopes and dreams out on display
My fears and depression viewable for everyone to
    see
And all the lack of happiness revealed
It's that part where they see how I just keep
    pushing through
Though I have no desire to get anywhere
It's that time they all finally found out
That I'm nothing more than a broken empty shell
All the jokes and laughs are all an act fooling
    those who don't really care to see.
Every smiles just as fake as the last
Yet I still forcefully paint it on myself
In truth I fill myself with darkness never truly
    caring if it goes away
But when I met you something lit a spark in me
And to this day I don't know what I regret more,
    never chasing it or letting it give me hope.

Let me hear you say you love me one last time
Let this world disappear and let it be the end of
    time
I care not for the future where I must walk alone
I care nothing for a past and a present with no
    home
For the wind has died and the grass no longer
    grows
The leaves have turned black and the doors have
    all been closed
The heart beats soften as I hear the last remnants
    of your voice
And then I think of the day we met and how I
    made the right choice

I walk these streets alone as the storms are
    outside
Matching my emotions of rage and sorrow
Each day gets darker clouds block out more of
    the sun
The bright blue sky has turned into nothing more
    than fantasy
I'd wish for a hand to hold or a warm embrace
    with no avail
No one can be found that would even give me
    the chance
They say I'm not they're type or I'll never be
    within a million years
Yet they haven't even looked at who I could really
    be
And each day as the sun should set, these clouds
    get darker and more violet
And the storms will one day flood away
    everything I am, and drown me in a sea of
    apathy

I don't know how much longer I can hold this
    back
A darkness so great it blacks out the blue sky
A pain so great it makes hell seem soothing
An ocean of tears so vast it would be an endless
    voyage
But I'll try to trudge on
Walking as steady as I can
I'll put on that fake smile to put you at ease
And put up an act that I fear I won't be able to
    end

Give me one good reason why I shouldn't
  disappear
I simple fact that should keep me grounded here
In a place that holds nothing in a way for my
  future
In a town that's so slow and will never get faster
If I were to leave it wouldn't be noticed
Or at most people would see me gone but I
  wouldn't be missed
I haven't left a mark or will I ever try
It's over for me with a roll of the dice
With the snake eyes up my image will fade
And that won't matter because soon, like
  everyone else, you will forget that day

They say when one door closes many more open
But I'm too hurt to even stand
With the darkness closing and the air starting to
    chill
I feel the tears drip down to my hands
With each breath I take my body gives up
I release all my feelings to the dark
And with all my pain finally gone and my eyes
    open wide
I realize I've been living so long without a heart

And it no longer means anything
As I drift off to sleep apathetically
With dreams that should hurt but I don't feel
their sting
With a cold breeze through my window but I
don't feel the wind
I've been numbed to the pains no matter what
they are
And my heart stops its fluttered beating when I
see our shared star
Since in the end it was only one way feelings for
you
As you left me in the darkness thinking the light
is never true.

I can take a hit and get back up
A left hook to the jaw makes me laugh
You can push me around and kick me while I'm
   down
But I'll still get up and press on
But at the days end there will always be
   something that can bring me to my knees
It's waking up alone, especially after these nightly
   dreams

Look me in the eyes and don't back down
Look me in the eyes and try to stand your ground
Don't run away when you finally see it
Don't try to understand every detail you see
There are things about me no one will ever know
And its people like you that judge me before the
    fact
So just shut the hell up unless you can see it in
    my eyes
The one thing no one bothers to look at, the true
    me.

Printed in the United States
By Bookmasters